LIVING IN THE FLOW

REMINDERS FOR A
SUPREMELY HAPPY LIFE

Craig Steven Phillips

For Information:
Tao Tribe Books
Telephones: 714-366-9097
Email: ZenGypsy@mac.com
Website: CraigStevenPhillips.com
Tao Tribe.com

ISBN: 1539789187
ISBN-13: 978-1539789185

*This book is dedicated, with great Love,
to everyone in the Tao Tribe.*

Contents

Forward: *What is the Flow?* 3

Prologue: *A Boat on a River* 11

1 *You Are Not Your Mind* 13

2 *It's Always Now* 17

3 *Live in the Flow* 21

4 *Be Still and Breathe* 25

5 *Everything Changes* 29

6 *Enlightenment Means
   "Lighten Up"* 33

7 *When in Doubt,
   Do Nothing* 37

8 *Act Without Doing* 41

9 *Enjoy the Ordinary Moments* 45

10 *Nothing "Out There" Will
    Make You Happy* 49

11 *Stay Balanced on the Tightrope* 53

12 *Let Others Be* 57

13 *Keep Your Agreements* 61

14 *You Are What You Eat*   65

15 *Move Your Body Now*   69

16 *Ask the Great Question*   73

17 *Be Grateful For All of It*   77

18 *Remember Where You Come From*   81

And in the End:

The Three Keys To Happiness   85

Epilogue:

The Monk, the Tiger and the Strawberry   89

Aloha and Goodbye:

Your Life is Your Message   91

FORWARD:
WHAT IS THE FLOW?

If we are honest, all of us are looking for greater peace and happiness in our busy lives. Yet in today's modern world, we can easily be overwhelmed by the sheer amount of information coming at us from all directions, and the speed at which everything is constantly changing.

Increasingly, we are left feeling cut off from ourselves and each other - tied into knots, and drowning in a sea of fear about what might happen tomorrow or next year, all while trying desperately to keep our heads above water.

With the realization that there is no security to be found anywhere, feelings of worry and fear have become commonplace and created an overwhelming sense of anxiety and unease in a majority of people. Many now experience this state of anxiety as the norm and devise endless strategies to deal with it; including 'doing more' as a way of avoiding the truth that, the more we do, the more exhausted and out of balance our lives feel.

From deep inside we are called to a simpler life, where everything flows with greater ease and harmony. We long to be free of the constant feelings of worry and fear that plague us, and to experience greater happiness that is not dependent on how much we do or what we have.

So it was for me back in 1988 when I stumbled upon a little book that would not only change my life forever, but also become my most trusted friend and advisor. That little book, called the Tao Te Ching (pronounced Dow Duh

Jing, which means, The Book of the Way and It's Power), has been my constant companion for over 28 years, and it's wisdom and guidance have served me more profoundly than any other book, spiritual or otherwise, that I have ever read.

"But what," you may ask, "is the Tao?"

Most of us are familiar with the old expression, 'go with the flow', and we could say that this is a perfect definition (as if it could ever be defined!) of the Tao.

It is the Universal Source that is giving rise to everything and everyone that you see around you (including you).

There is *nothing* you can do, be, or conceive that doesn't originate in the Tao.

It is the producer, director and all of the actors in this great drama of life, and yet is mysteriously *beyond* and untouched by all that It allows to happen.

It flows as the eternally present moment - the way of things, *as they are,* here and now.

It is simplicity itself.

Look around you; all that you see has it's life in the Tao, and without It, you wouldn't even know that you exist; that's how magnificent It is.

And the Tao Te Ching, that little book of 81 verses that I mentioned earlier, written 2800 years ago by a wise old sage named Lao Tzu, remains a user-friendly manual on how to align yourself with, and live in the flow of, this great Universal Intelligence, while really enjoying the ride. After all, isn't being happy and joyful what we truly want?

Though it took me many years to realize that the Tao Te Ching's simplicity was it's greatest strength, when I first discovered it's teachings (or should I say, *they* discovered me), I wasn't quite ready to accept that living a life of happiness and freedom could be as easy as it proposed.

After all, I was used to a life of trying to control everything that happened, and resisting everything that I thought shouldn't be happening, all the while noticing that everything that *actually* happened was beyond my control anyway.

These endless attempts to try and force life to be the way that I thought it should be were; not only futile; but incredibly exhausting.

I spent my days filled with worry and fear, was quick to anger; full of judgement, and far away from actually living my life in the effortless flow that the Tao Te Ching said was possible.

Yet deep inside, something had clicked.

I knew intuitively that what I had read was not only possible; but more importantly, it was the only way to find the kind of peace and happiness that I longed for.

Despite this, I wasn't quite ready; I still needed more 'seeking', more teachers, more books, more retreats, and a more complicated process so I could work out this elusive state of 'enlightenment' that I so desperately craved.

Through years of frustration and endless spiritual pursuits, the teachings of the Tao Te Ching kept resurfacing in my life, calling me to return to the simplicity of the present moment, where the state of freedom and happiness that I longed for waited for me as surely as my breath.

Finally, after years of running around in circles, and enduring the suffering that was my constant companion, there came a day when I felt so lost and exhausted that I couldn't even remember what it was that I had been seeking. At that point, I found myself open to the realization that everything was as simple as what the Tao Te Ching first promised; that letting go of trying to control what can't be controlled and surrendering completely to *what is*, leads to the peace and tranquility that is always available in the present moment.

All that was needed was to open my eyes, actually *see* what was in front of me, and break-off the love affair I had with the stories in my head about what *should* be happening.

I discovered that the flow I had spent years looking for had always been available, waiting for me to simply wake-up and come home to the here and now. All that needed to be done was to let go of the mistaken belief that fulfillment was going to be found elsewhere, in some future time when the conditions were right; and I had done enough to earn it. I found that there was *nothing* I had to do to be who I already am; and in this discovery it was seen that; who I am; is already complete.

And if your mind starts to protest that all of this sounds too simple, well, can the simple truth be too simple?

It is the embracing of this simplicity, and a willingness to *deeply relax* and wake up to the present moment, *as it is,* that frees us from looking 'out there' in the world; for the fulfillment that can only be found within. Everything then becomes intuitively obvious, and what had once been over-looked, reveals itself again, as if for the first time.

The little book that you're now reading, born out of years of applying the teachings found in the Tao Te Ching, along with the regular practice of meditation, Qigong and Tai Chi, contains reminder's that will assist you in living a life in the effortless flow of the Tao.

Put what you're about to read into practice in your daily life, and what you will re-discover is the harmony and balance that leads to the flow within your own Being, where everything unfolds with the greatest of ease. Living in, and as this flow, you also re-discover the happiness and freedom that you have always known were possible, but had temporarily forgotten.

The invitation to you as you begin this book, is to surrender your resistance to whatever shows up in your life, and instead to look upon everything that happens as a gift from the Universe (Tao) that is for your greatest benefit. Trust that the journey of your life is taking you exactly where you need to go, at exactly the time you need to be there, so that you can learn to live in the perfect flow of the Tao.

After all, whatever is to happen in your life is going to happen anyway, with or without your approval, so why not relax, celebrate and enjoy the scenery along the Way?

A note about how to use this book: I suggest going through the chapters in chronological order the first time and allowing each one to sink in deeply. After that, use the book as a source of guidance for wherever you may find yourself each day. The 18 chapters are meant as helpful pointers for any problem or challenge you may face, or can be used as meditation's to move you into the flow.

If you're feeling adventurous, write or type out the numbers 1 through 18, cut them into squares, and put them into a container.

Each day, or whenever you feel confusion or uncertainty in your life, pick a number and read the corresponding chapter. You may find that the wisdom you receive is exactly what you need for whatever situation you're facing.

"Flow with whatever is happening
and let your mind be free.
Stay centered by accepting
whatever you are doing.
This is the ultimate.

- Chuang Tzu

PROLOGUE:
A BOAT ON A RIVER

Coming into this world is like finding yourself at the edge of a powerfully flowing river. On it's banks you find a row boat has been placed there to help you navigate the current.

Though the direction of this rushing river is moving *downstream,* you convince yourself that happiness and peace can only be found *upstream.* So, you take a seat in the boat and immediately turn it around and begin rowing furiously against the current, believing that fulfillment awaits you *in the future,* in a place just around the next bend.

Though you begin to sweat, struggle and lose your breath, you tirelessly press on, with little joy or happiness to show for your efforts.

Year after year, decade after decade, you continue to fight against this powerful flow, until finally, mercifully, you find yourself in a space of such exhaustion and despair, that you have *no choice* but to let go of your dream of ever reaching the destination you have spent your entire life *trying* to reach.

Yet, in the very moment of *letting go,* to your amazement, your boat begins to turn itself around and move *downstream,* in the direction the river is actually going. You soon find yourself sailing along with more effortless ease than you have ever known, with more joy than your heart has ever felt. With all of the struggle now gone, you are actually able to enjoy each moment of the journey, and all of the scenery along the way.

So easy becomes your life in the flow, that you eventually throw your oars overboard and put your complete trust in the river to take you where it will.

Gone are the attempts to get to some specific location where you think you can find happiness, and instead, there is the realization that, wherever you are *right now*, is exactly where you need to be.

As you live out the remainder of your life, immersed in, and trusting the flow, you remember a song that you learned as a child, but whose meaning had alluded you during all those years of struggle. As you sing it out loud, to no one in particular, it becomes the embodiment of living a happy and awakened life....

"Row, row, row your boat
gently down the stream.
Merrily, merrily, merrily, merrily,
life is but a dream."

1 YOU ARE NOT YOUR MIND

Are you familiar with the loud voice that is constantly playing in your head?

The running commentary that incessantly judges, doubts and resists everything that happens to you; and within you? The voice that repeatedly assures you that it has your best interests at heart, yet always seems to end up causing more frustration and suffering when you follow it's advice? This 'voice', often referred to as the mind or ego-consciousness, is the identity that most human beings believe themselves to be.

Yet, what if it turned out that this voice in your head wasn't you at all, but instead, a great impostor that you have falsely taken yourself to be? Wouldn't that be the greatest news that you could receive?

With just a little investigation and curiosity, we can begin to see for ourselves that this complaining and fearful ego, with it's feeling of being separate from everyone and everything else, is not who we are at all. Nor are we the hurricane of thoughts that always seem to accompany it.

Thankfully, who and what we are is way more simple and easy to know: *we are that which is listening to, and watching, the activity of the mind.*

Please don't take my word for this; look for yourself.

As you think about one thing or another, isn't it true that 'you' *know* what the mind is thinking - that 'you' are the one who is listening to the thoughts playing in your head?

Relaxing deeply we can see that there are thoughts in the mind, and there is also 'me' who is listening to the thoughts. After all, how else would we know what we are thinking?

This 'watcher' of the mind knows what is being thought, yet is not the thoughts themselves. This knower of the mind, often referred to as Awareness or Witness-Consciousness is your own true nature.

Try this little experiment for yourself - close your eyes and repeat the words, *"I am not the mind'* to yourself several times.

Contemplate for a moment who it is that is *listening* to this thought. Who is it that *hears* the thought? Look deeply and be there as the one *listening* to the mental activity while relaxed in the body, but be sure not to 'think' about what you discover, as that is simply more thoughts appearing in the mind.

What you may begin to re-discover is the simplicity of what you truly are; the awareness that *listens* too, and *knows* what the mind is thinking. In fact, this Awake-Awareness is looking through your eyes and *knows* what is being seen, hears through your ears and *knows* what is being heard, and feels through your hands, *knowing* what is being felt.

Without this Awake-Awareness, you would not *know* anything; it alone is the *knower* of all you experience.

To rest as this simple Awareness is the purpose of all true spiritual practice. Living as this Awareness gives rise to the experience of freedom and happiness that we have been looking for our entire lives, and brings us home to who we are, here and now.

Tao Practice: Close your eyes and bring this question to your mind; "*Who is it that is listening to my thoughts?*"

Instead of immediately trying to answer the question with more thinking, relax and allow the answer to arise from beyond the mind, and rest as the wordless Awareness that is listening to the question itself.

As you relax into the knowing of what you are, bring this question to your mind, "*Before my next thought, who am I?*"

"Here is it - right now.
start thinking about it
and you lose it."

\- Huang Po

2 IT'S ALWAYS NOW

Have you ever noticed that it's always Now? That no matter what you do or where you go, it's always taking place in the space we call the 'present moment'?

In fact, if you contemplate deeply, you will find that your entire life has unfolded in the here and now, and you have never left it for even a second. However, you may have also noticed that the mind isn't very interested in the Now, but instead, loves to think about the past and future, what happened yesterday or what may happen tomorrow.

It loves to speculate on a wide variety of problems and outcomes that may, or may not occur, all of which are imagined. Yet the simple, undeniable truth is that there is no past or future; there is only and ever the present moment.

Let that really sink in; there is no past or future, there is only this moment, right now.

If we look clearly, even the thoughts we have about the past and future are taking place in the here and now.

When we think about something that happened last year or reminisce about something that happened in our childhood, we do so presently. Likewise, when we find ourselves projecting some future scenario or worrying about what may happen tomorrow or next year, we do so right now.

People can spend their entire lives so preoccupied with the past and future, that they never touch down in the actual space where their whole lives unfold: the eternal present.

Like sleep-walkers who are unaware of what is happening around and within them, most human beings go to their graves without ever having been *awake* to the beauty of life. No wonder so many people come to the end of their days feeling as if they have never lived at all.

The point of all spiritual teachings and techniques are to awaken us to this truth; that the open space of the here and now is all there ever is and ever will be. This wonderful discovery allows us to enjoy and be present to what is actually unfolding right in front of us and frees us from trying, in vain, to be somewhere else. We also find that, when we stop resisting whatever is happening, and instead, relax and *flow with it*, our lives begin to unfold with the effortless ease and freedom for which we have always longed.

In letting go of our habitual struggle with the present moment, we find that it is never the events of our lives, but instead our thoughts about those events, that cause us to suffer.

When we bring ourselves fully to the eternal Now, we move into harmony with the *way things are* and into the current of the Tao, which is always moving in exactly the right direction.

By living in this ever-flowing perfection, we begin to appreciate life in all it's fullness; the smile of a cherished friend, the sun shining through the leaves of a tree, or the ecstasy of our favorite song..

As we stop being adversarial toward life, and instead welcome everything that shows up as if we had chosen it, we find that life starts to be friendly toward us, and every moment holds the opportunity for delight. The question is always; *are we actually here* to enjoy it?

Tao Practice: Whenever you find yourself worrying about the future or obsessing about the past, take a refreshing breath and actually pay attention to where you are right now.

Look through your eyes and see what's there; listen to whatever sounds are arising, and open to what is actually unfolding right in front of you.

Feel the space around and inside your body and bring this question to your mind, 'what problem do I have, right now'? Notice that in the space of the present moment, where your whole life unfolds, there are never any problems to solve. No matter how many times your awareness gets swept away into the river of thought, and thus into the illusion of past and future, keep coming back.

Realizing that you're not present means that you are present once again.

Keep waking up out of the dream of the mind and it's constant projections into the future. In this way you come into alignment with the Tao; the effortless, flowing reality of the present moment, *as it is.*

3 LIVE IN THE FLOW

You've probably noticed that you don't have a lot of control over what happens to you. For instance, one moment you're driving along, merry as can be, and the next thing you know, someone has smashed carelessly into your new car. Or one day you are experiencing perfect health and the next day you find yourself in the hospital with a life-threatening illness.

Just as we know that we don't have any control over

whether the sun rises each morning, we eventually come to realize that we simply don't have the control over our lives that we wish we did.

If we look deeply, we don't even have control over our thinking in the way we believe we do. After all, do you know what your next thought will be? Don't thoughts just seem to happen of themselves?

Life has a way of showing us, again and again, that despite our attempts to control what happens to us, we just don't have the ability to make things unfold in the way we want them to.

In fact, there are really only two apparent choices we can make when it comes to the events of our lives; either to resist what happens, and thus create internal suffering and unhappiness, or to accept and move in harmony with whatever occurs, knowing that it is happening for our complete benefit.

Going with the flow of life doesn't mean that we throw up our hands and allow events to roll over us as if we have no power to affect change. On the contrary, this flowing *with* the current of Life (the Tao), instead of opposing it, always gives us the ability to meet any challenge that may appear with clarity and wisdom, without depleting ourselves with needless worry and anxiety in the process.

It also gives us a deep peace, acceptance and humor as we allow the next step on our journey to reveal itself to us at just the right time; with the least amount of effort.

All that is required is to be willing to let go of the illusion of control, and surrender to the flow of the Tao, which is *always* moving us in exactly the right direction.

Tao practice: When you notice any resistance or sense of struggle with whatever happens today, take a refreshing breath and remind yourself that you are exactly where you are suppose to be. After all, where else could you be?

Notice that it is your resistance to what happens that creates the feelings of anxiety and tension in your life, and never the actual events themselves. Repeat to yourself, on a regular basis, "I am surrendered to the perfect flow of the Tao," trusting that *everything* is happening for your highest good.

*"You should sit in meditation
for at least 20 minutes a day,
unless you're too busy -
then you should sit for an hour."*

- Zen Saying

4 BE STILL AND BREATHE

"Be still like a mountain
and flow like a great river."

Lao Tse Tung

As the world around us becomes increasingly chaotic and uncertain, our lives can often seem out of control, and peace of mind as fleeting as a dream. Often we can feel like we are sleepwalking through life, barely aware of what is actually going on around, and within us.

As we wake-up from the illusion that anything 'out there' in the world will ultimately satisfy us, we can find ourselves looking for a way to experience the contentment and peace that our hearts long for.

Interestingly, one of the things that almost all of the world's spiritual traditions agree upon is the power of daily meditation to bring tranquility to our minds and happiness to our hearts.

Mindfulness, which is the current (ancient) buzzword for meditation, is once again being touted in the media as a valuable practice for bringing our busy mind back from it's constant wandering into the past and future, to the reality of the here and now.

The practice of meditation gives us the opportunity to relax out of the 'monkey mind', the voice in our head that is constantly worrying, judging, complaining and trying to get anywhere but here.

Even more important than the well-documented health benefits of daily meditation, increased energy, alleviation of anxiety, and improved sleep (among many others); we find that when we turn within for even as little as 10 minutes a day, we begin to touch down in the peace and stillness that are at the heart of our true nature.

As we make it our practice to actually *be present* with whatever is unfolding here and now, we find ourselves living from this Awake-Awareness. We also find that we begin to enjoy *all* of the activities of our life, and experience happiness in even the most ordinary moments; whether it's washing the dishes, working in the garden, or taking care of our children.

Reminding ourselves to take three refreshing breaths every hour will do more to improve the quality of our life than all of the time we squander mindlessly engaged in activities that distract us from the present moment. All that is required to know the freedom and clarity of your true nature is to begin a meditation practice and to stay with it, no matter how much the mind may try to convince you that you have better things to do.

If happiness and peace are what you truly want, you don't.

Tao Practice: Here is a very simple meditation technique that you can practice daily. Start with 10 minutes, increasing to 15 or 20 minutes, twice a day.

Find a quiet place where you won't be disturbed and sit upright, either on the floor or in a chair.

The point here is to be comfortable; you don't need to be rigid or stoic in your posture, but relaxed, with a feeling of openness toward the present moment.

Get a sense of relaxing into the space around your body and allow everything to be *as it is*, without trying to make anything 'special' happen through your meditation.

As you feel a sense of openness to *what is*, bring your awareness to your breathing, feeling it as it flows through your nose and down to an area three inches below your navel, right in the center of your body.

This area, known as the Tan Tien (The Field of Heaven or Elixir Field), can be imagined as a luminous golden-red sphere about the size of a softball, which fills up when you inhale and empties on your out breath. Don't worry if you have a hard time visualizing this; *feeling* it is much more important.

After a couple of minutes of breathing this way, gently bring your awareness to the middle of your head, and get a sense that you are sitting in an old ancient cave; what the old Taoist Masters call the *cave of original spirit*. From this point, lift your interior gaze up as if you're looking out through your forehead into a vast open sky, and gently bring your attention to you're breathing as it flows in and flows out.

Notice that, as the breath reaches it's peak, there is a slight pause before it turns and goes out again. Let yourself rest in that little space between your in and your out-breath - that is the domain of your true nature; Awareness Itself.

If you become caught up in thinking again, which may happen, gently return your attention to your breathing and gaze once again into the big-sky of your own relaxed Being.

A little something extra: If you find that your mind is giving you a lot of trouble, and settling down is difficult, then begin repeating a word; such as *calm, peace, love* or any other word that you resonate with, on your out-breath. After 10 minutes, or however long you wish to meditate, let go of all technique, and simply sit in the silence and stillness that has arisen through your practice.

If peace and joy are what you wish to experience on a regular basis, then repeat daily, if possible (and it's always possible).

5 EVERYTHING CHANGES

*"If you realize that all things change,
there is nothing you will try to hold on to"*

Tao Te Ching

If you have lived long enough, you already know the truth
that everything in life eventually changes and ends.

Relationships, jobs, places where we live; one day all of
these will inevitably change and give way to something
new. This also includes our bodies, all of our experiences
(both good and bad), and even our thoughts. Though we
know the truth of this, we can find ourselves holding on

tightly to what is passing from our lives, and in this grasping we create a lot of unnecessary pain and suffering.

If we look deeply, we will notice that this holding on never stops the changes we are resisting from happening anyway, but only serves to create more suffering and unhappiness.

The good news is that, when we look back at everything that we have gone through in our lives, we might find that all of the changes that have occurred have always led to something even better: the ending of an unhappy relationship becomes the new romance; losing a job that is unsatisfying leads to the career that we have always dreamed of.

How many times have we gone through challenging circumstances that, at the time, were painful and seemed to take something from us, yet after a few months or years turned out to be the best thing that could have happened?

The point is this; everything that happens is *always* the best possible thing that can happen, but only if we are willing to let go of our resistance, and open to the gifts that every transition inevitably brings.

By embracing the truth that change is an inevitable part of life, we free ourselves to actually enjoy what is happening right now, without the unrealistic expectation that it should last forever.

In fully accepting that whatever comes eventually goes, and flowing *with* these changes instead of opposing them; we find ourselves aligned with the current of the Tao; and living with a greater peace and happiness in our lives.

Tao Practice: Take a moment to contemplate a time when something; a relationship, a job, a valued possession suddenly changed or was taken from you. Although you may have felt sadness, betrayal or unhappiness at the time, what was the result of this loss after a year? What about five years?

Open yourself to the truth that every change that you go through always leads to something better, if you're willing to open and see.

*"The only difference
between a wise man
and a fool
is that the wise man
knows he's playing."*

- Fritz Pearls

6 ENLIGHTENMENT MEANS 'LIGHTEN UP'

We've all been there.

We find ourselves facing an impossible situation that has been building for weeks; planning, worrying, and struggling with the possible outcomes that may, or may not, occur. As we become increasingly heavy and serious, we feel unable to enjoy even the briefest respite from what's troubling us. Then one day, right in the middle of this mental torture, a question arises within you that brings your mind to a full stop.

"Does this *really* matter," you ask yourself, and all at once you realize, in the grand scheme of things, it doesn't matter at all.

Out of this realization you find yourself laughing at the absurdity of what you have been putting yourself through, at how 'serious' you've been taking it all. In that moment of laughter and relief you 'lighten up' and all of the heaviness you've been carrying around with you suddenly begins to fall away.

Though this feeling of lightness and freedom may only last a few moments, you notice that the situation you had once taken to be so pressing and important; suddenly begins to clear up in the process of life itself.

Despite our exhausting attempts to control what happens to us, our life keeps relentlessly unfolding exactly as it does.

Many people believe that they will reach a point in the future where there won't be any more challenges, and they will be endlessly happy and blissful. Of course, no matter what we do, this long-sought after state of security never seems to materialize, except for brief moments when we satisfy some cherished desire and get what we want. But this kind of satisfaction is always temporary and, in the end, not very fulfilling.

Yet, what if the happiness we are looking for in these experiences, including spiritual enlightenment, is simply about *lightening up*, here and now, and recognizing that nothing ultimately matters in the way our mind thinks it does?

Just notice that when you start to feel heavy and serious about any situation you're going through, the solutions to those challenges are as elusive as the happiness and peace that you long for.

Conversely, when you let go and lighten up; remembering that everything is always working out for your complete benefit, you find yourself in the very heart of happiness, where the solutions to the problems you face reveal themselves effortlessly, in the natural flow of your life.

Tao Practice: When facing any kind of challenge today, take a refreshing breath and ask yourself, "Does this *really* matter?"

Take a moment to allow yourself to gain some perspective.

If you still feel that it does matter, then ask yourself if it will be important a year from now? How about 5 years? Contemplate the truth that, every difficult situation you have ever faced has eventually dissolved and vanished, and whatever you are going through now will do the same.

"Praise and blame,
gain and loss,
pleasure and sorrow,
come and go
like the wind.
To be happy,
rest like a giant tree
in the midst of them."

- Buddha

7 WHEN IN DOUBT, DO NOTHING

"Let go -
or be dragged."

Zen Saying

So there you are at a crossroads, with two paths leading in two different directions. No matter how much you think about your dilemma, you simply don't know what to do.

You can't eat and you can't sleep, and it feels as though you have come to your wits-end. You've asked for advice from your family and friends, meditated for days; you've even consulted a psychic, and you still don't know which way to turn. In these moments of confusion and uncertainty, what if the answer to your problem was not in doing something, but in doing nothing?

What if you simply allowed yourself to feel the confusion fully, and flowed with not knowing what to do? What if you took the imagined pressure off of yourself, enjoyed a refreshing breath and allowed everything to be as it is?

When people ask you what you've decided to do, you can smile and say, "Oh nothing. I don't know what to do, so I'm not going to do anything."

The opposite of this approach, and the one that most people follow, is to rush in, swinging wildly, trying to do something, anything to alleviate the confusion; and in the process, creating even more uncertainty and suffering.

In giving ourselves completely to our indecision however, we might find that the solutions to the challenges we face arise in their own way and in their own time. It's only when we force ourselves to make a decision, even though we may not be ready to do so, that we find ourselves regretting our choice and lamenting the unhappiness that results.

The point is, when in doubt, do nothing.

Have the patience to wait until your confusion settles down, and the right course of action is revealed to you, and then follow it with all of your heart. You might be delightfully surprised at how many of the challenges you encounter just seem to clear up in the process of life itself, without you having to do anything at all.

And when action is required, if it comes out of this clear and patient space, you will find that it always results in everything working out wonderfully well for you, with the least amount of effort on your part.

Tao Practice: Whenever you feel conflicted or confused about any decision you need to make in your life, give yourself a day to let things settle down before acting. If you still feel uncertain, take another day or even a week if necessary. What you will discover is that the indecision you feel gives way to the perfect choice for you to make, without you having to do anything to make it happen.

*"Stop trying to control;
let go of fixed plans and concepts
and your life
will unfold by itself."*

- Tao Te Ching

8 ACT WITHOUT DOING

We experience the Tao, the effortless unfolding of the present moment, when we let go of our habitual struggle and resistance to the direction life is moving in, and allow ourselves instead to, 'go with the flow'.

One of the easiest ways to do this is through the Taoist practice of Wu Wei, which means; 'doing without doing', as in having all your needs met while exerting the least amount of effort and energy as possible. From another perspective, it's getting our ego-mind, with it's need to control every aspect of our lives, out of the way, and allowing Divine Intelligence (the Tao) to do the heavy lifting.

Of course this runs counter to the prevailing wisdom (madness?) of the world, which tells us that we need to sweat, worry and do 'something, anything', to make things work out the way we think they should.

In this constant state of tension and unease, we tie ourselves into knots, thereby cutting ourselves off from the creative energy that we need to bring our plans and goals to fruition. We also deplete ourselves of the very joy and enthusiasm that make life worth living in the first place.

The good news is that we can drop this exhausting struggle anytime we choose by simply aligning ourselves with the direction that our lives are already moving.

When we stop trying to manipulate life into giving us what we think will make us happy, and instead begin to follow the intuitive promptings of our heart, we discover an effortless doing that always leads us to the perfect circumstances for our happiness.

We are then able to take action that produces results without the struggle, anxiety and frustration that usually accompanies our doing.

With struggle now gone, we rediscover the happiness and enthusiasm that is always at the heart of all creative activity, and in the process, actually begin to enjoy our lives again. We also find that the more we stop our compulsive 'doing', the more we find that the path we are looking for is the one right under our feet.

Tao Practice: As you go through your day, simply respond to whatever the Tao (Life) brings you. Instead of trying to further your plans and agendas, let yourself flow with whatever presents itself to be done, and respond accordingly. Let go of constantly trying to exert your will; and instead; take a step back and let the Tao lead the dance.

*"The clouds above us
join and separate.
The breeze in the courtyard
leaves and returns.
Life is like that,
so why not relax?
Who can stop us
from celebrating?"*

- Lu Yu

9 ENJOY THE ORDINARY MOMENTS

Often we can find ourselves waiting for something extraordinary to happen in our lives.

We dream of doing great things; writing a best-selling novel, climbing Mt. Everest, or perhaps creating something that changes the course of human history. We tell ourselves that we simply won't be happy or satisfied till we are recognized the world over for our unique talents, or at least have a million hits on Youtube. Few of us however, have the destiny to be the next Mother Theresa or Dalai Lama, let alone Steve Jobs.

In our waiting for those events that we think will make us feel that our lives are meaningful, we often miss out on the ordinary, beautiful moments that make up the bulk of our lives; walking through a garden, seeing a movie with friends, or relaxing with a favorite beverage.

In our endless craving to be somewhere else or something more than we are right now, we miss out on the brilliance of life, in all it's crazy glory. If we are willing to open our eyes to what is happening right in front of us, here and now, we can begin to see *every* moment as a gift.

The truth is that, what we think of as the extraordinary moments of our life - the wedding, the trip around the world or winning the lottery - make up a very small portion of our time on earth. It is the ordinary, mundane events that will make up the vast majority of what we do while we are here.

The question is always, are we actually present right now to enjoy these ordinary moments as they occur, or are we 'waiting' for something better to show up?

In this continual state of waiting for a more fulfilling life in the future, there may come a day when we realize that we haven't really lived at all.

Tao Practice: Be fully present to the ordinary activities of your life today. Whether it's washing the dishes, grocery shopping or driving to work; be there fully with whatever you are doing.

Whenever you find yourself waiting or wishing for something better than what is happening right now, take a refreshing breath and bring your awareness back to the gift of the present moment Repeat to yourself on a regular basis, "There is only Now, there is only the Tao."

*"The only Zen you will find
on the mountaintop
is the Zen you take
up there with you."*

- Zen Saying

10 NOTHING 'OUT THERE' WILL MAKE YOU HAPPY

Perhaps you have spent the majority of your life believing that something out in the world will make you happy - that if you just had the right job, the right amount of money in the bank, or the right relationship, you would be eternally joyful and your life would have the meaning you think it should. Yet you may have noticed that, when you do get what you want, the satisfaction you experience is temporary at best, and it isn't long before the mind, once again, begins to look for something else 'out there' to fulfill it's deep-seated feeling of fear and lack.

Despite having been told by every spiritual teacher and philosopher since the beginning of time that the fulfillment we long for cannot be found in anything outside of us, we can still find ourselves clinging to the belief that there is something or someone 'out there' who will do the trick. We hold out the hope that the next big thing in our lives will finally bring the happiness we are looking for.

Yet again and again, the simple truth keeps hitting us in the face; nothing in the world will ever give us the lasting peace and fulfillment we long for.

If we know this, why not just save ourselves from this continual frustration, and drop the illusion once and for all? Why not begin to focus on the one place where you can find the treasure of happiness that you so desperately long for; the space *within you*?

When we come home to ourselves in the present moment, we find the contentment and peace that we have spent our whole lives searching for. We also find ourselves more fully appreciative of the blessings that already fill our lives.

When we realize that *everything* we want is already available within us, we easily re-discover the joy and happiness that we have always known were possible. When we are truly present, we find that the here and now, *as it is*, is already enough, and there is never anything lacking in our lives.

Tao Practice: Whenever you notice that you are looking for something out in the world; a relationship, a possession or any experience to make you feel more complete and fulfilled, take a refreshing breath and ask yourself this question, "Here and now, is there anything lacking?"

Listen deeply for the answer; and make it your practice to come back to this question throughout the day. What you may find is that, in the present moment, there is never anything lacking, and the more you focus on this feeling, the more it begins to grow in you.

"When walking,
just walk.
When sitting,
just sit.
Above all -
don't wobble."

- Linji

11 STAY BALANCED ON THE TIGHTROPE

The high-wire artist knows that he must stay completely focused on the step he is taking or he will lose his balance and fall to his death. In the same way, each of us are walking a tightrope called life, doing our best to keep our balance in the midst of life's twists and turns.

We all know what it feels like to lose our balance - that moment of exhaustion when we feel depleted of vital energy as we needlessly worry about a future event or find ourselves regretting something that happened in the past.

Perhaps we aren't getting enough sleep, eating to much junk food or not getting enough physical exercise.

If we are honest, every area of our life has a balance point where we feel harmony within, and with the world around us. Conversely, there is also a tipping point where we feel out of balance and begin to experience stress, anxiety and unease.

All that is required to bring ourselves back into harmony with the flow of the Tao, is to spend some time doing the practices that bring us back into balance (meditation, qigong, yoga, healthy eating).

By being honest with ourselves and focusing on those areas of our lives that need our attention, we naturally return to a state of radiant health and abundant energy. As we develop the wisdom of knowing when we are out of balance, we can immediately take the steps necessary to regain our footing once it has been lost.

This is very good news.

One of the most empowering gifts of living in the present moment is that we realize our well-being is our own responsibility. We wake up from the dream that anything 'out there' in the world can cause our pain and suffering; and find ourselves making choices that bring greater balance to our lives. As we move into greater harmony with the current of the Tao, we naturally avoid activities and relationships that drain our vital energy (Qi).

By avoiding the extremes in any situation, and living with inner-balance, we find ourselves right in the center of a powerful flow that it always unfolding our lives with the greatest of ease.

Tao Practice: Make a list today of three areas in your life where you feel balanced and at peace. Then make a list of three areas where you feel out of balance, and compare the two. Ask yourself what you need to do to bring *all* areas of your life into harmony.

Whether is it needing to get more rest, eating a more healthy diet, doing some meditation, or watching less T.V., choose just one area of your life where you are out of balance and spend a little time today giving some attention to it. Trust the wisdom of your heart to guide you.

*"Many paths lead
from the foot of
the mountain
but, at the peak,
we all gaze at the
single bright moon."*

Ikkyu -

12 LET OTHERS BE

Have you ever noticed that, while we often have no clue about what to do with our own lives, quite magically, we believe that we know exactly what others should do with theirs?

Often unsolicited, we offer our sage advice to anyone who will listen, and do so with an air of authority that belies our own confusion and uncertainty. In our self-righteousness, we often push away our family and friends with our pontifications about the course their lives should take, alienating them even further with our insistence that our guidance is the only course of action for them to take.

If we are honest however, we can never know what's best for someone else, despite our belief too the contrary.

Seen from another perspective, we can always know that whatever a person is doing at any given moment is exactly what they need to be doing. How can we know this? *Because it's what they're doing!* We can know that wherever they find themselves always holds the perfect lessons for their growth and evolution.

From this way of looking, everything that happens is always unfolding perfectly for their highest good, no matter how we may judge it otherwise. And of course, this is true not only for others, but for ourselves as well.

When others know they can trust us to listen without prejudice, it frees them to find the perfect solutions to the challenges they face and allows us to be there for them without our judgements getting in the way. It also allows us to listen with compassion, which is simply knowing that everyone (including ourselves) are doing the best they can.

When we realize that we can never know what is best for someone else, and simply accept them as they are, we open a space for true relationship to flower; and the possibility for true love to unfold.

Tao Practice: Notice any compulsion you may have to give advice to anyone today. Before doing so, take a refreshing breath and ask yourself, "Can I really know what's best for this person?" Then listen deeply; holding them in a space of compassion, while allowing them to be as they are. Know that, just like you, they are doing the best that they can and are exactly where they need to be for the next step of their own learning and growth.

*"It is no sign
of mental health
to be well adjusted
to an insane life."*

- Dalai Lama

13 KEEP YOUR AGREEMENTS

*Life works to the degree
that you keep your agreements."*

Werner Erhard

It has been said that 98% of all human suffering is created by people not keeping their agreements with each other.

Though it may not be considered a 'spiritual' quality, keeping our commitments with others is actually the foundation to living a happy and authentic life. Saying what we mean and meaning what we say, people know that they can count on us to do what we say we'll do, and not do what we say we won't. When we break our agreements with others, we undermine our own integrity, and not only will other people no longer trust us, we will no longer trust ourselves.

In todays world, it is commonplace for people to break their commitments without a care about the repercussions it has on their relationships with others and themselves.

Yet the truth is that, until we learn to keep our word under all circumstances, we will never be able to completely trust ourselves to follow through on anything we say we'll do, and we will end up sabotaging our own happiness at every turn. We will also end up living our lives in a constant state of guilt and regret over the way we have let others, and ourselves, down.

If you find that keeping your agreements with others is difficult, one of the things you can do to make it easier, is to simply stop making commitments that you don't really want to make. For instance, when someone asks you to do something, like helping them move or picking them up from the airport, you can take a refreshing breath; and ask yourself if you really want to do what's being asked of you. If you don't, then simply say 'no' and this will save you from having to make an excuse later on, when you end up breaking your agreement.

When you agree to do anything for another person, let it arise out of a feeling of actually *wanting* to do it, rather than from a feeling of wanting to please them or because you would feel guilty for saying no.

The main thing to ask yourself before making any agreement is, do you have the intention to follow through on what you say you'll do or will you end up flaking out,; and perhaps cause hurt feelings in the process? When you no longer do things because you feel obligated to do them, and instead do them because you genuinely want to do them, your life will begin to feel authentic and you will be filled with happiness and peace.

This alone will end most of the broken agreements in your life and a large majority of the drama you put yourself through. Without this drama, you will find yourself at ease, and living in the perfect flow of the Tao.

Tao Practice: Can it really be true that all we need to do to have a life that is in harmony with the present moment, is to keep our word and do what we say we'll do? Find out today by making only those agreements that resonate with your deepest integrity, letting go of any feeling of 'should' or guilt that may arise. What you may find is that your life becomes, not only easier, but also happier in the process.

"The best doctors are:
Dr. Diet, Dr. Quiet
and Dr. Merry-man."

- Jonathan Swift

14 YOU ARE WHAT YOU EAT

There are a million healthy eating plans out there. By now, unless you've been living under a rock on the moon, you know what constitutes a heathy diet, and what you need to eat to live with energy and vitality.

When you boil down all of the thousands of nutritional books and diet plans that have been written, what you find is simply this: if you eat crap you will feel like crap, and if you eat healthy food, you'll feel vibrantly alive. Let's be honest, it's not rocket science; we all know that an apple is better for us than a candy bar, a glass of pure water more invigorating than a soda, a colorful salad more life-sustaining than a side of bacon.

Each of us already has the wisdom to know what we need to put into our bodies to experience optimum health and energy, the question is, do we have the commitment to do so?

If you don't, why not just admit it and begin to notice how you feel when you make the choice to put something unhealthy into your body? If you really listen, chances are you'll feel very quickly how fast food makes you feel heavy and tired, while a meal of vegetables, beans, whole grains and fruit leaves you feeling light and energized.

Remind yourself before you eat the next bite of junk food that you do have a choice; before you pop the next can of soda, ask yourself, "Do I really want to feel like crap today?"

From this simple question, allow yourself to make the choices that lead to optimum health and well-being; and the energy and vitality that are the result.

Tao Practice: If you find that there are changes you wish to make to your diet, start with one thing first - perhaps giving up soda and drinking more water instead, or replacing dairy with a substitute like almond or rice milk. Don't attempt to make too many changes at once, as this will probably overwhelm you and only lead to eating even more unhealthy.

The key is to pay attention to how the food you eat makes you feel. Actually notice which foods make you feel heavy and lethargic, and which ones make you feel vibrant and energized. Make your choices based on this awareness.

15 MOVE YOUR BODY NOW

The number one New Years resolution for most people continues to be to lose weight and get into shape. So, on Jan. 2, gyms everywhere are filled to capacity as millions of would-be Ninja Warriors hit the treadmill, the elliptical trainer and the stationary bike, huffing and puffing with steely determination, and finding very little joy in what they are doing. Is it any wonder that, by Feb. 1, most of those who had been working out, tell themselves that they deserve a much needed rest; and so begin to skip exercise sessions to recuperate?

Then, by the time March rolls around, well, there's always next year, isn't there?

This reminder, like the one about eating, is simple and straightforward. It's a well known fact that, if you wish to feel good on a consistent basis and experience radiant health, you have to move your body (o.k., you don't 'have' to, but you might want to, if feeling good is something you wish to do on a regular basis).

Just as with the millions of diet books that have been published, there are also countless exercise regiments out there that promise to turn you into a ripped god or goddess in as little as two weeks. Yet, exercise programs, like diets, will work till you get bored, tired, or convince yourself that something else is more important, even if that 'something else' is sitting in front of the T.V. watching reruns.

The answer to this madness is to simply move your body in a way that you actually enjoy, and do it at least five times per week, no matter what. Whether it's walking, yoga, water aerobics, qigong, running, tennis or biking (or a combination of these), pick something, anything that you find enjoyable and stick with it no matter what excuse the mind may throw at you.

Enjoyable is the key word here. After all, you're not likely to stick with anything for very long if you don't enjoy doing it.

Developing the discipline to continue, no matter what, is also a major element to being in shape, and will lead to the radiant health and abundant energy that you long for. And if, for whatever reason, you get lazy and stop for awhile; instead of beating yourself up, simply begin again, over and over if you must, for the rest of your life.

Tao Practice: Move your body today. Begin by doing 15 minutes of some activity that you enjoy; walk around the block, take a yoga class, enroll in a water aerobics or qigong class. The point is, do something, anything that gets your body moving at least five times per week. The results, increased energy, lower blood pressure and better sleep; will be all the motivation you need to continue.

*"I have no power of miracle
other than the attainment
of quiet happiness.
I have no plan
except the exercise
of gentleness."*

- Sumiyoshi

16 WHAT DO YOU REALLY WANT?

"The Great Way is easy,
yet people prefer the side paths."

Tao Te Ching

A great question to ask ourselves from time to time is, "What do I *really* want in my life, right now?"

Often, there can be a huge gap between what we say we want and what we actually experience in the present moment. For example, we may say that we really wish to be at peace, and may even tell anyone who will listen that it's what we want more than anything in the world. Yet, in the next moment we can find ourselves acting out in ways that lead, not to peace, but to more confusion and sorrow.

There's nothing wrong with this of course, but we may notice that it's not very satisfying, and ends up making us feel even more lost and confused.

We can spend our whole life wrapped in a story who's main character is bent on finding some kind of happiness and fulfillment, only to find ourselves in yet another self-created misadventure that leads to more unhappiness and suffering.

The key to becoming free of this unconscious pattern is to make it conscious, and simply be honest about what we really want in our lives.

One thing is certain, when we truly want something (i.e. peace, joy, calmness, freedom), and are willing to align everything we do in our lives to having it, then it will begin to show up almost immediately. In fact, we may be delighted to discover that we have always had what we most long for; that we had simply forgotten that it has always been a part of us.

Though we are often looking for answers to the challenges in our lives, what we might begin to notice is that it is often the questions we ask ourselves that open us up to the wisdom and clarity that we most need at any given moment.

Tao Practice: Close your eyes and take a refreshing breath. As you relax deeply, bring this question to your mind, "What do I *really* want in my life, right now?"

Bring this wish to just one word. For example we may long for more calmness in our life, so with great focus and intention, repeat the word *calm* on your out breath for several rounds. What you may notice is that the *experience* of the word you are repeating begins to arise within you quite naturally.

Begin to focus on what you *really* want in your life throughout the day and align your actions, words and thoughts with this one wish. What you will notice is that the experience of what you most want begins to arise within, and around you, more quickly than you can imagine.

"If the only prayer
you were to ever say
was 'thank you' -
that would be enough.

- Meister Eckhart

17 BE GRATEFUL FOR
ALL OF IT

*"Contentment is found in the realization
of how much you already have."*

Zen Saying

We can spend the majority of our lives focused on getting what we think will make us happy. We tell ourselves that we will only find contentment when we 'do this' or 'get that'. Even when we do manage to fulfill a cherished desire, we are often left with the feeling that something is still missing., and it isn't long before the mind convinces us that happiness will be found in the attainment of yet another desire. This continual pursuit of something out in the world often leaves us feeling empty and void of true satisfaction in our lives.

Yet, as the Zen proverb teaches, the surest and quickest way to feel happiness and fulfillment is to simply recognize, and be grateful for, the abundance and blessings that already fill our lives.

This can be done by taking the time each day to pause, look around you, and feel gratitude for what is happening right now; a beautiful sunset, a bite of delicious food, the laughter of a child or the breath you're taking.

By paying attention and opening our hearts to what is actually happening right now, we will begin to feel joy that is not dependent on anything being a particular way.

In fact, we will begin to feel gratitude for *everything* that shows up in our lives, knowing that it is happening *for us; that it contains the exact lessons that we need, at this moment, for our own growth, and thus, for our own happiness.*

Of course, gratitude is easy when things seem to be going our way. But true happiness can only be experienced on a regular basis when we are willing to see *everything* that shows up in our life as a blessing, no matter how difficult it may seem at the time. After all, everyone has gone through hardships that, at the time, were painful but turned out to be the best thing that could have happened. When we remember this, we can begin to fully appreciate, not only the pleasant moments, but also the apparent times of adversity.

As we open to being friendly toward life, we begin to notice that life becomes friendly toward us. This leads to being delighted with *everything* that happens, knowing it is always unfolding for our highest benefit.

Tao Practice: Before going to bed this evening, write down three things that happened today that you are grateful for. This can be as simple as the first sip of your morning coffee or an unexpected phone call you received from a good friend. Do this everyday for three weeks and you may begin to notice how appreciative you feel for even the most mundane events of your life. Notice how this appreciation leads to even more blessings to be grateful for.

"If someone asks my abode
I reply: The east edge of
the Milky Way.

Like a drifting cloud,
bound by nothing:
I just let go.
Giving myself up
to the whim of the wind."

\- Ryokan

18 REMEMBER WHERE YOU COME FROM

There are very few things that we can know for sure in this life, but one thing we can count on with all certainty is this: one fine day, probably when we least expect it, we are going to depart this earth.

It is an indisputable fact that you, and everyone you know, will come to the moment when you draw your last breath and depart on the wings of your last exhalation. Yet, many people live their entire lives in denial of this simple truth. Overwhelmed by the very thought of death, they try to avoid even mentioning the word for fear that it may bring on the dreaded occasion.

Despite all of the evidence of it's reality, facing our own mortality can leave us with a feeling of anxiety that cuts us off from truly living.

However, many spiritual heavyweights, including the Buddha, have said that death can be one of our greatest teachers, reminding us that our time on this earth is limited, and to use the days we have remaining to wake up to who and what we are. It's message to us is to focus on what is truly important in our lives and to let go of the stuff that doesn't ultimately matter (and just about everything that we think matters, really doesn't in the end).

Death reminds us to enjoy what is right in front of us, knowing that it is not going to last forever. In fact, the most important lesson that our mortality teaches us is to wake up to the here and now; and enjoy the ordinary moments of our lives.

It is in paying attention to these ordinary moments that we discover life's rich pageant - the endless kaleidoscope of colors, sounds, feelings and experiences that make up the total of our days on this planet. In this way, we also begin to see that time is a fleeting illusion, and that life passes by in the 'wink of an eye'. The question is always, are you actually here to enjoy it?

Tao practice: Ask yourself if you have truly been alive today. Did you actually do what brought you happiness and joy, or are you 'waiting' for some future moment, when the time is 'right'. Contemplate what it is that you really want in your life, and look and see if you are putting it off for another day. Fully accept that your life is not forever, and that the future you envision may never come at all - that all you ever have is *this moment* to wake up and enjoy the gift of your precious human birth.

*"Life pretty much comes down
to just three things:
Everything changes
Everything is connected
Pay Attention!*

- Jane Hirshfield

AND IN THE END:
THE THREE KEYS TO HAPPINESS

As we come to the end of our little journey together, just remember that there are only three things that you will ever need to know in order to be happy and peaceful for the rest of your life. Of course, we have already covered these three 'keys' in the chapters of this book, but it's always helpful to remind ourselves as often as possible of what is essential to living a life in the effortless flow of the Tao.

So once again, here are the three essential teachings that are the basis for living a joyful existence. Though your mind may try to convince you that living with freedom and ease cannot possibly be this simple, don't be fooled. Everything boils down to the realization of these three truths:

Truth #1: You Are Not Your Mind. This is the most vital and important truth that you will ever hear: no matter how much you may believe otherwise, you are not, nor will you ever be the voice in your head. You are, and will always be, the Awake-Awareness that is watching and listening to the mind.

The erroneous identification with the running commentary in your head, like a case of mistaken identity, is the root cause of all the suffering and misery you will ever experience in your life. To break free from this mind-created hypnosis, take time throughout the day to ask yourself this question, "Who, or what, is listening to my mind?"

Don't bother looking for an answer in yet another thought, but instead, breathe deeply into the space that opens up when you ask the question.

This open, sky-like Awareness is who you are beyond the constant stream of mental activity - that which is simply watching and listening to the mind. To live from this Awareness, from the depth of who you really are, is the point of all spiritual practices and teachings, and is the only thing that will bring the happiness and freedom that your heart longs for.

Truth #2: Your Whole Life Will Unfold in the Here and Now. Let this really sink in: there has never been, nor will there ever be, a time when you will not be in the Now. Though you may spend most of your life thinking about the past or worrying about the future, the truth is, you will never spend one moment of your life actually visiting either of those mind-made locations.

The present moment is the only space in which you will ever be alive, so why not wake-up to this reality and begin to appreciate what is happening right now? Don't waste the remainder of your precious life living in a dream of regret about what happened yesterday or worrying about what may happen tomorrow. Open your eyes, come to your senses, and see what is actually in front of you right now, and embrace the gift of this moment, *as it is*.

Truth #3: Everything Changes and Ends. Within the space of the here and now moment, everything is constantly changing. If we are honest, nothing stays the same for very long, no matter how much we may wish otherwise.

Peace and contentment arise when we completely accept this truth and learn to flow with the changes that occur, rather than resisting and fighting them. It is this inner resistance, and the attempts to hold on to what is passing from our lives, that creates all of the suffering and misery that we experience.

When we stop clinging to what is passing, and instead let go and open up our hands, we are then in a position to receive the new blessings that are always flowing into our lives from the Tao.

THE MONK, THE TIGER
AND THE STRAWBERRY

Once upon a time there was an old Taoist Master named Tao Ji who was walking home to his monastery in the Wudang mountains. As he enjoyed the sunshine of a beautiful spring day, the Master was set upon by a ferocious tiger.

Running for his life, the old man was driven to the edge of a very high cliff. Knowing that if he jumped it would mean certain death, Tao Ji saw a short vine that was growing down the side of the mountain, and with the angry cat nearly upon him, took it in his hands and lowered himself over the edge.

As the old man contemplated his predicament, he noticed that two field mice, one white and one black, had begun gnawing at the vine that tethered him to the side of the cliff. Looking down he saw that yet another tiger was waiting below, should he fall. In the midst of this dilemma, the Master's eyes alighted on a wild strawberry growing out of the side of the mountain.

"Ah, yes!" the old man exclaimed with delight.

Taking the vine in his right hand, he reached out with his left and, plucking the ripe fruit, brought it to his mouth. As the mice gnawed through the last remaining threads of the vine he was holding, the Master took a bite of the most delicious strawberry he had ever tasted.

"This is it!
There are no hidden meanings.
All of that mystical stuff
is just what's so.
Not so obviously,
it's also - so what.
A Master is someone
who found out."

- Werner Erhard

Aloha and Goodbye

"Your life is your message to the world."

Thich Nhat Hanh

Living in the perfect flow of the Tao, and experiencing the happiness and peace that is the result, is the greatest adventure that we will ever undertake. It is also the only thing that will ultimately bring the joy and fulfillment that we long for in our lives. All that is required of us is to make the commitment to be awake in the present moment; and no matter how many times we may get side-tracked by the drama's of the mind, to return to it again and again.

This is also the greatest contribution we can make to the peace and happiness of others, and to the survival of the planet. When we are actually *here and now*, we are better able to choose those actions that serve and uplift all beings, while also bringing greater peace, compassion and kindness into the world. In the end, we learn that serving and being kind to others is the fast-track to the happiness that we long for.

In fully trusting the Source that is behind this vast, magical play of life, we easily find the peace and contentment that we have spent our whole lives searching for. It is my deepest wish that everyone reading this book may learn to live in harmony with the unending and eternal flow of the Tao; and come home to the sanctuary of the present moment. After all *"If not Now, when?"*

About the Author:

Craig Steven Phillips is a Taoist/Buddhist teacher and author who has been practicing and teaching meditation, Qigong and Tai Chi for the past 36 years. He considers the day he came across the *Tao Te Ching* as the most auspicious moment of his life.

Besides being a preposterous rascal, he is also an Interfaith Minister and was ordained into Buddhism by the Dalai Lama. You can find out more about his classes and events at: CraigStevenPhillips.com or TaoTribe.com

Recommended reading:

Mitchell, Stephen, *Tao Te Ching.* New York: Harper Perennial, 1988

Walker, Brian, *Hua Hu Ching.* San Francisco: Harper Collins, 1992

Tolle, Eckhart, *The Power of Now.* Novato, Ca. New World Library, 1999

Katie, Byron, *A Thousand Names for Joy,* New York, N.Y., Harmony Books, 2007

Thich Nhat Hanh, *Peace is Every Step,* Bantam Books, 1992

Thich Nhat Hanh, *You Are Here: Discovering the Magic of the Present Moment,* Boston, Massachusetts, Shambhala Publications, 2001

Singer, Michael, *The Untethered Soul,* Oakland, Ca. New Harbor Publications, 2007

Adyashanti, *Falling Into Grace,* Boulder, Co., Sounds True Publishing, 2011

Adamson, Sailor Bob, *What's Wrong With Right Now, Unless You Think About It?,* Mumbai, India, Zen Publications, 2001